MODERN-DAY
PROVERBS

Truths to live a life that is
happy, joyous, and free

Juris S.

ISBN 978-1-63814-677-3 (Paperback)
ISBN 978-1-63814-678-0 (Digital)

Copyright © 2021 Juris S.
All rights reserved
First Edition

The excerpts from Alcoholics Anonymous, the Big Book are reprinted with permission of A.A. World Services, Inc. ("A.A.W.S."). Permission to reprint these excerpts does not mean that A.A.W.S. has reviewed or approved the contents of this publication, or that A.A.W.S. necessarily agrees with the views expressed herein. A.A. is a program of recovery from alcoholism only—use of these excerpts in connection with programs and activities which are patterned after A.A., but which address other problems, or in any other non A.A. context, does not imply otherwise.

All rights reserved. No part of this publication may be reproduced, distributed, or transmitted in any form or by any means, including photocopying, recording, or other electronic or mechanical methods without the prior written permission of the publisher. For permission requests, solicit the publisher via the address below.

Covenant Books, Inc.
11661 Hwy 707
Murrells Inlet, SC 29576
www.covenantbooks.com

Table of Contents

1. Drowning in Information,
   Starving in Wisdom 5
2. Definitions 11
3. Spiritual Truths 41
4. Practical Truths 71
5. Action Truths 97
6. Emotional Truths 137
7. Relationship Truths 161

Drowning in Information, Starving in Wisdom

Life, liberty, and the pursuit of happiness.

The Declaration of Independence, written over two hundred years ago, states that human beings are "endowed by their Creator certain unalienable rights that among these are life, liberty, and the pursuit of happiness." Yet today, why is it that we live in an age where happiness is so elusive? Rates of depression, alcoholism and addiction, and suicide are climbing at alarming rates, especially in recent years. Happiness and satisfaction in the United States are trending downward, not upward.

In our internet age, there is a plethora of information that is being pumped into the universe. The sad fact about this is that the vast majority of it is not true. Many people go through every day without hearing or reading a single thing that is actually true. This leads to a delusional belief system which drives individuals to actions which are not beneficial to themselves or others, leading to despair, hopelessness, and destruction to themselves and society. We are drowning in information, but starving in wisdom.

Truth is immutable, meaning that it never changes and that it cannot be changed. It applies to all people, in all situations, and at all times. It does not care about how you feel. It does not care where you are from. It does not care who your parents are. It does not care what language you speak, or what color your skin is. It does not evolve or change with the times. It is the truth.

Truth may not be understood sometimes, but that doesn't make it any less true. Truth may not feel like the right thing to a person, but that does not make it any less true. Truth may even seem completely contradictory to a person's logic, but that does not make it any less true.

Going against truth will never satisfy a person's spirit, even if in the moment, it seems like it will. Going against truth will never lead to joy, even if a person believes that it will, and even if the world is condoning and encouraging it.

DROWNING IN INFORMATION, STARVING IN WISDOM

This has been my experience as well as my observation of many, many people's experiences. The majority of people are on a happiness quest. They are looking for whatever makes them happy in the moment. "Do whatever makes you happy." "If it makes you happy and you are not hurting anyone else, then it's okay." But from my observation, that way of living only ends in destruction.

If you want to be truly happy, if you truly want to have joy, if you truly want freedom, you need to be on a truth quest, not a happiness quest. Not only finding the truth, but applying it and living it out daily. It will never let you down because the truth never changes.

It really is that black and white. You can argue with it. You can fight it. You can ignore it. You can learn it and not use it. No matter what you do with the truth, what is will always be what is. It either is or it isn't. It does not need to be understood. It needs to be accepted and used appropriately. That's it.

It's simple, but it is not easy. Truth sometimes doesn't make sense to the human mind and emotions. In fact, a lot of truth is counterintuitive. It is illogical based on our patterns of thinking. It is in direct opposition to much of what the world would teach you and have you believe.

The following pages contain simple yet profound, practical, spiritual truths and wisdom that I have found can lead to overwhelming freedom, joy, and happiness. I particularly like them because they are short and easy to remember. These truths will affect a person in different ways, depending on the condition of their heart at the moment and other circumstances in life. However, the one thing that never changes is the impact of these truths on a human being and his or her ability to relate to the world and enjoy it.

Meditate on these truths. Look for how these can be applied to your life. Look back on your experiences and see where these truths surfaced, and what the result was. When a situation arises, you will start to remember these truths, and apply them to your life. Write down your experiences when you practice these truths. Discuss these truths with others. Remember, these things do not need to be understood to be used. They merely need to be accepted and applied.

This is by no means comprehensive, but it serves as a powerful tool to lead the best life that you possibly could lead—the life that God has ordained for you. You can fulfill your ultimate destiny, which has been pre-determined by the creator of the universe, and not of yourself. The results will blow you away. You will achieve and gain more than you ever dreamed you could. You will look at your life over time and realize that you had never seen, heard, or imagined anything as beautiful as the way your life unfolds over time.

You have no idea how magnificent, enjoyable, and satisfying your life can be.

DEFINITIONS

DEFINITIONS

"Our real purpose is to fit ourselves to be of maximum service to God and the people about us."

(Alcoholics Anonymous, 4th ed., 77)

MODERN-DAY PROVERBS

Life without purpose is punishment.
Life with purpose is passion.

DEFINITIONS

"There is a principle which is a bar against all information, which is proof against all argument and which cannot fail to keep a man in everlasting ignorance. This principle is contempt prior to examination."

(Herbert Spencer)

MODERN-DAY PROVERBS

"There's no normal life. There's just life."

(Doc Holliday to Wyatt Earp in *Tombstone*)

DEFINITIONS

Comparison is the thief of joy.

MODERN-DAY PROVERBS

Expectations are future resentments.

DEFINITIONS

Wisdom is the ability to make Godly choices.

MODERN-DAY PROVERBS

Love is service to another person,
expecting nothing in return.

DEFINITIONS

Insanity is doing the same thing over and over and expecting a different result.

MODERN-DAY PROVERBS

Integrity is doing what is right
when no one is watching.

DEFINITIONS

Pride is thinking that we are better than another person.
Shame is thinking that we are worse than another person.
True humility is knowing and believing that every person on earth has the exact same value.

MODERN-DAY PROVERBS

One characteristic of humility is the continual willingness to be taught.

DEFINITIONS

Sarcasm is anger's evil twin.

MODERN-DAY PROVERBS

Forgiveness is releasing someone else's emotional control over me.

DEFINITIONS

Surrendering is not losing.
Surrendering is joining the winning team.

MODERN-DAY PROVERBS

One definition of addiction is continued use in the face of adverse consequences.

DEFINITIONS

The opposite of addiction is connection and community.

MODERN-DAY PROVERBS

"A real man-1) rejects passivity, 2) accepts responsibility, 3) leads courageously, and 4) lives for a calling greater than himself."

(Robert Lewis)

DEFINITIONS

All of our problems today are illusions (they have not happened yet). Our problems today are opportunities.

MODERN-DAY PROVERBS

Every addiction begins as the pursuit of pleasure and ends with the avoidance of pain.

DEFINITIONS

Every rock bottom has a trap door.

MODERN-DAY PROVERBS

Every hope has a fear behind it.

DEFINITIONS

Ego cannot exist in the present moment because ego is all about what you have done or what you are going to do.

MODERN-DAY PROVERBS

Perfect is the enemy of good.

DEFINITIONS

Complacency is gratitude without service.

MODERN-DAY PROVERBS

It is never the wrong time to do the right thing.

DEFINITIONS

"We are here to add what we can to,
not get what we can from, life."

(Sir William Osler)

SPIRITUAL TRUTHS

SPIRITUAL TRUTHS

What you believe when you think about God
is the most important thing about you.

MODERN-DAY PROVERBS

"One can easily understand a child's fear of the dark, but what is the greatest tragedy in life is the grown man who is afraid of the light".

(Plato)

SPIRITUAL TRUTHS

It's not God's will that makes us miserable.
It's our resistance to God's will
that makes us miserable.

MODERN-DAY PROVERBS

No God, no peace.
Know God, know peace.

SPIRITUAL TRUTHS

Every sinner has a future.
Every saint has a past.

MODERN-DAY PROVERBS

"Maximum freedom in your life comes from submission to authority."

(Brady Cooper)

SPIRITUAL TRUTHS

"Human nature says, 'I will believe it when I see it.' Faith says, 'I will believe it, and then I will see it."

(Joel Osteen)

MODERN-DAY PROVERBS

On the other side of our greatest struggle, is our greatest blessing.

SPIRITUAL TRUTHS

God provides the most healing at the intersection of honesty, humility, and truth.

MODERN-DAY PROVERBS

We are not judged by our intentions.
We are judged by our actions.

SPIRITUAL TRUTHS

The pain of discipline is less
than the pain of regret.

MODERN-DAY PROVERBS

"The unexamined life is not worth living."

(Socrates)

SPIRITUAL TRUTHS

"You seek to imitate the kind
of God you believe in."

(Gregory Boyles)

MODERN-DAY PROVERBS

God has to take us through it to take us to Him.

SPIRITUAL TRUTHS

"Religion is for people who're afraid of going to hell. Spirituality is for people who've already been there."

(Vine Deloria)

MODERN-DAY PROVERBS

The blessing doesn't flow to us.
The blessing flows through us.

SPIRITUAL TRUTHS

"It is the heart that makes a man rich.
He is rich according to what he is,
not according to what he has."

(Henry Ward Beecher)

MODERN-DAY PROVERBS

"Beware the barrenness of a busy life."

(Socrates)

SPIRITUAL TRUTHS

We cannot transmit something we do not have.

MODERN-DAY PROVERBS

"Education of the mind without an education of the heart is no education at all."

(Aristotle)

SPIRITUAL TRUTHS

Every action is based in either fear or love.

MODERN-DAY PROVERBS

You cannot keep what you have
unless you give it back.

SPIRITUAL TRUTHS

God is good all the time.
And all the time, God is good.

MODERN-DAY PROVERBS

"A Bible that is falling apart usually belongs to someone who isn't."

(Charles Spurgeon)

SPIRITUAL TRUTHS

"Free people free people.
Hurt people hurt people."

(B. Haley)

MODERN-DAY PROVERBS

We are not bad people trying to be good.
We are spiritually sick people trying
to become spiritually healthy.

SPIRITUAL TRUTHS

A clear conscience is a good pillow.

MODERN-DAY PROVERBS

"Every man lives by faith, the nonbeliever as well as the saint; the one by faith in natural laws and the other by faith in God. Every man throughout his entire life constantly accepts without understanding."

(AW Tozer, *The Knowledge of the Holy*)

PRACTICAL TRUTHS

PRACTICAL TRUTHS

"The strength of a nation lies in
the homes of its people."

(Abraham Lincoln)

MODERN-DAY PROVERBS

"A system of morality which is based on relative emotional values is a mere illusion, a thoroughly vulgar conception which has nothing sound in it and nothing true."

(Socrates)

PRACTICAL TRUTHS

No is a complete answer.

MODERN-DAY PROVERBS

Experience is the best teacher.

PRACTICAL TRUTHS

"One moment of patience may ward off a great disaster; one moment of impatience may ruin a whole life."

(Chinese Proverb)

MODERN-DAY PROVERBS

"A man who has committed a mistake and doesn't correct it is committing another mistake."

(Confucius)

PRACTICAL TRUTHS

"Great minds discuss ideas; average minds discuss events; small minds discuss people."

(Eleanor Roosevelt)

MODERN-DAY PROVERBS

Successful people never worry
about what others are doing.

PRACTICAL TRUTHS

"He who can take advice is sometimes superior to him who can give it."

(Karl Ludwig von Knebel)

MODERN-DAY PROVERBS

More is caught than taught.

PRACTICAL TRUTHS

Our children follow our example, not our advice.

MODERN-DAY PROVERBS

"Train up a child in the way he should go—
but be sure you go that way yourself."

(Charles Spurgeon)

PRACTICAL TRUTHS

What parents tolerate in moderation,
children will excuse in excess.

MODERN-DAY PROVERBS

We can either be humble or we will be humbled.

PRACTICAL TRUTHS

Encouragement is like an oasis in the desert.

MODERN-DAY PROVERBS

Yesterday's recovery is as good
as yesterday's shower.
Yesterday's prayer is as good as yesterday's shower.

PRACTICAL TRUTHS

"What day is it?" asked Pooh. "It's today!" said Piglet. "My favorite day," said Pooh.

MODERN-DAY PROVERBS

Movement benefits the body.
Stillness benefits the mind.

PRACTICAL TRUTHS

Some days we are the windshield.
Some days we are the bug.

MODERN-DAY PROVERBS

Losing is not failure if used as feedback.

PRACTICAL TRUTHS

Life is about progress, not perfection.

MODERN-DAY PROVERBS

The journey of a thousand miles
begins with one step.

PRACTICAL TRUTHS

Random acts of kindness garner
temporary benefit.
Intentional acts of kindness reap eternal rewards.

ACTION TRUTHS

ACTION TRUTHS

"Be the change you wish to see in the world."

(Gandhi)

MODERN-DAY PROVERBS

"If you want to bring happiness to the world, go home and love your family."

(Mother Theresa)

ACTION TRUTHS

"The best preparation for tomorrow is
to do today's work superbly well."

(Sir William Osler)

MODERN-DAY PROVERBS

"Life isn't about waiting for the storm to pass.
It's about learning how to dance in the rain."

(Vivian Greene)

ACTION TRUTHS

"The spiritual life is not a theory.
We have to live it."

*(Alcoholics Anonymous, 4*th *ed., 83)*

MODERN-DAY PROVERBS

We cannot think our way into right acting.
We must act our way into right thinking.

ACTION TRUTHS

You cannot fake showing up.

MODERN-DAY PROVERBS

"Miraculous turns of fate can happen to those who persist in showing up."

(Elizabeth Gilbert)

ACTION TRUTHS

Don't quit before the miracle happens.

MODERN-DAY PROVERBS

It is easier to do the next right action
than to explain why you didn't.

ACTION TRUTHS

What you allow will continue.

MODERN-DAY PROVERBS

You will never run out of excuses
but you will run out of time.

ACTION TRUTHS

If you want self-esteem, do estimable acts.

MODERN-DAY PROVERBS

If you want something to happen in
your life, pray for someone else.

ACTION TRUTHS

If we want something we have never had,
we have to do things we have never done.

MODERN-DAY PROVERBS

The workout is not the one hour in the gym. The real workout is controlling what's on the plate the other 23 hours of the day.

ACTION TRUTHS

If you don't say anything, you can't say the wrong thing.

MODERN-DAY PROVERBS

Don't speak unless you can improve the silence.

ACTION TRUTHS

Don't worry about calming the storm.
Calm yourself.
The storm will pass.

MODERN-DAY PROVERBS

Watch your thoughts, they become words; watch your words, they become actions; watch your actions, they become habits; watch your habits, they become character; watch your character, for it becomes your destiny.

ACTION TRUTHS

Better than yesterday.
Worse than tomorrow.

MODERN-DAY PROVERBS

Don't just do something, stand there.

ACTION TRUTHS

"Do or do not. There is no try."

(Yoda)

MODERN-DAY PROVERBS

If you hang out in a barbershop long enough, you will eventually get a haircut.

ACTION TRUTHS

```
            Clean house
                 △
               /   \
              /     \
             / Pick  \
            /  two    \
           /_____\
   Happy kids        Your sanity
```

MODERN-DAY PROVERBS

You will not have lasting prosperity
if you do not have integrity.

ACTION TRUTHS

Going to church does not make you a Christian any more than sitting in a garage makes you a car.

MODERN-DAY PROVERBS

You are to blossom where you are planted.

ACTION TRUTHS

"There are only two kinds of people in the end: those who say to God, "Thy will be done," and those to whom God says, in the end, "Thy will be done." All that are in Hell, choose it. Without that self-choice, there could be no Hell. No soul that seriously and constantly desires joy will ever miss it. Those who seek find. Those who knock it will be opened."

(CS Lewis, *The Great Divorce*)

MODERN-DAY PROVERBS

Every morning in Africa, a gazelle wakes up. It knows it must run faster than the fastest lion or it will be eaten. Every morning in Africa, a lion wakes up. It knows it must run faster than the slowest gazelle or it will starve to death. So it doesn't matter if you are a lion or a gazelle, when the sun comes up, you better be ready.

ACTION TRUTHS

"Don't judge each day by the harvest you reap but by the seeds that you plant."

(Robert Louis Stevenson)

MODERN-DAY PROVERBS

We are either working on recovery
or we are working on relapse.

ACTION TRUTHS

The secret to abundant living
is the abundant giving.

(Caveat—if you are getting paid
for your service, it is not giving)

MODERN-DAY PROVERBS

"You have not lived today until you have done something for someone who can never repay you."

(John Bunyan)

ACTION TRUTHS

If you have one foot in tomorrow and one foot in yesterday, you are pissing on today.

MODERN-DAY PROVERBS

"The arrogance of success is to think that what you did yesterday will be sufficient for tomorrow."

(William Pollard)

ACTION TRUTHS

"Be happy for this moment. This moment is your life."

(Omar Khayyam)

EMOTIONAL TRUTHS

EMOTIONAL TRUTHS

It is impossible to be grateful and resentful at the same time.

MODERN-DAY PROVERBS

Don't be sad that it's over.
Be happy that it happened.

EMOTIONAL TRUTHS

Be ~~with~~ someone who makes you happy.

MODERN-DAY PROVERBS

Focus equals feeling.

(What you choose to focus on will directly impact how you feel)

EMOTIONAL TRUTHS

Feelings are not facts.

MODERN-DAY PROVERBS

"To cure jealousy is to see it for what it is, a dissatisfaction with self."

(Joan Didion)

EMOTIONAL TRUTHS

The pain is inevitable.
The suffering is optional.

MODERN-DAY PROVERBS

Attachment is the root of all suffering.

EMOTIONAL TRUTHS

Two of the most powerful, healing words
in the English language are, "Me too."

MODERN-DAY PROVERBS

"Secrecy is the enemy of intimacy."

(Dave Willis)

EMOTIONAL TRUTHS

No one cares how much you know until they know how much you care.

MODERN-DAY PROVERBS

Underlying all unrighteous (selfish) anger is a non-acceptance of God's will.

EMOTIONAL TRUTHS

You are only as happy as your unhappiest child.

MODERN-DAY PROVERBS

Your family knows how to push your buttons because they are the ones who installed them.

EMOTIONAL TRUTHS

Food is the most abused anti-anxiety drug.
Exercise is the most under-utilized antidepressant.

MODERN-DAY PROVERBS

"If you do not have peace on the inside,
you will not have peace on the outside."

(Joel Osteen)

EMOTIONAL TRUTHS

"I love you doesn't mean you love me.
It means I love you."

(Dan Mohler)

MODERN-DAY PROVERBS

"Love is something if you give away,
you end up having more."

(Malvina Reynolds)

EMOTIONAL TRUTHS

"No one can make you feel inferior
without your consent."

(Eleanor Roosevelt)

MODERN-DAY PROVERBS

"Truth without love is brutality, and love without truth is hypocrisy."

(Warren Wiersbe)

EMOTIONAL TRUTHS

If you want happiness for an hour, take a nap. If you want happiness for a day, go fishing. If you want happiness for a year, inherit a fortune. If you want happiness for a lifetime, go help someone else.

(Chinese proverb)

MODERN-DAY PROVERBS

"You won't find happiness at the end
of a road named selfishness."

(Gary Thomas, *Sacred Marriage*)

RELATIONSHIP TRUTHS

RELATIONSHIP TRUTHS

Treat people the way you want to be treated.

MODERN-DAY PROVERBS

"The deception of others is nearly always rooted in the deception of ourselves."

(Bill W.)

RELATIONSHIP TRUTHS

When most people say, "For better or for worse," they just mean, "for better."

MODERN-DAY PROVERBS

The grass is not greener on the other side.
The grass is greener where you water it.

RELATIONSHIP TRUTHS

Our most important disciples are our children.

MODERN-DAY PROVERBS

"Teenagers who are doing well are not doing well because they have the right rules around them. Teenagers who are doing well are doing well because God has a hold of their hearts."

(Paul David Tripp)

RELATIONSHIP TRUTHS

"If you make sure someone else's life is all right, God will make sure your life is all right."

(Inky Johnson)

MODERN-DAY PROVERBS

"If you only live for yourself, you
will end up by yourself."

(Brady Cooper)

RELATIONSHIP TRUTHS

Helpfulness is the sunny side of control.

MODERN-DAY PROVERBS

The people about us are not an interruption to our days. They are the very reason for them.

RELATIONSHIP TRUTHS

You cannot rationalize with an irrational person.

MODERN-DAY PROVERBS

"The greatest good you can do for
another is not just to share your riches,
but reveal to him his own."

(Benjamin Disraeli)

About the Author

Juris S. was born and raised in Chicago, Illinois, and its suburbs. He is a grateful follower of Jesus Christ. He is a recovering alcoholic and addict, retired professional competitive eater, former model, and ordained deacon. His heart's desire is to share the truth in love to help others discover abundant, extravagant life. He is a board-certified orthopedic spine surgeon. He lives a life beyond what he had ever seen, heard, or imagined with his wife and four children in Tennessee.

CPSIA information can be obtained
at www.ICGtesting.com
Printed in the USA
LVHW020131070222
710103LV00007B/20